C000255500

Spiritual D
and Leadership
Formation

A Practical Exposition of Matt 3.13–4.11

Matthew Porter

Vicar of St Chad's, Woodseats, Sheffield

GROVE BOOKS LIMITED
RIDLEY HALL RD CAMBRIDGE CB3 9HU

Contents

Foreword

This book emerged out a series of seminars I led in various Rotherham churches during Lent 2004 and then subsequent Lay Training Days for the Diocese of Sheffield in Autumn 2004. I have been grateful for these opportunities to develop this fascinating and challenging subject.

All biblical references are taken from the New International Version (Inclusive Language) unless otherwise indicated.

The Cover Illustration is by Peter Ashton

First Impression July 2005
ISSN 1470-8531
ISBN 1 85174 597 1

Introduction   **1**

This Book Is...

This book is about the relationship between (what I have termed) the four discipline battles and leadership formation. It offers a fresh reading of Matthew 3.13–4.11, based on the battles Christ experienced in his will, body, mind and soul. It recognizes the special place of fasting in leadership formation and the importance of being led by the Holy Spirit. The church should take this seriously when encouraging leadership formation today.

This Book Is Not...

This book is not an expert treatise on the nature of leadership, fasting or spiritual discipline. Neither does it engage fully with the pertinent expository issues relating to Matthew 3.13–4.11. Assumptions are made concerning the reality of the Holy Spirit and the devil.[1] These raise a number of interesting theological, sociological and psychological issues; however, the devotional and practical nature of this text, coupled its brevity, do not allow me to develop these in any significant detail.[2]

Purpose

As I survey the contemporary church I see many leaders, particularly in the renewal movement, who have been empowered by the Spirit for leadership in God's church. Unfortunately I do not see many leaders who have embraced a life of discipline. This needs addressing, especially in the emerging generation of leaders.[3]

My simple hope is that this booklet will help future church leaders to learn from the leadership formation of Jesus Christ, who, led by the Spirit, and tested through various discipline battles, beautifully integrates a life of both freedom and discipline.

2

Leadership Formation and Spirit Empowerment

Leadership Formation

Leadership formation is the process of being formed for Christian leadership.[4] Christian leaders are, first and foremost, disciples of Jesus Christ. We cannot lead if we cannot follow. As we follow Christ's Spirit, where might he take us? He will lead us to all sorts of places, for the life of the follower is an exciting adventure. It is a spiritual journey that enables us to live life to the full, the way it was intended to be (John 10.10). This life of exploration will involve being stretched, challenged and developed as a person, some of which may not always seem comfortable at the time. Nevertheless, as we truly follow we learn, like the first disciples of old, that he knows what he is doing. The need for trust is paramount (Rom 15.13).

Into the Desert

There is one place that Jesus went that has always intrigued me: the desert. It seems like a strange place to go, especially just before he began his ministry. Why did he go there? What for? And what might that mean for me?

Jesus was tempted in the desert. Many, of course, see Jesus' temptations as something to be avoided if at all possible. For them, the temptation story offers examples of how to cope when temptation comes. But I am not convinced this is the main reason why God has left this story in the pages of Scripture, for it makes little sense of the Spirit actively leading Jesus into the desert.[5] This narrative teaches us about Jesus' leadership preparation,[6] and as such guides us in our leadership formation.[7] So we must reflect again on Matthew 3.13–4.11, and we begin with the first four verses.

> Then Jesus came from Galilee to the Jordan to be baptized by John. But John tried to deter him, saying, 'I need to be baptized by you, and do you come to me?' Jesus replied, 'Let it be so now; it is proper for us to do this to fulfil all righteousness.' Then John consented. As soon as Jesus was baptized, he went up out of the water. At that moment heaven was opened, and he saw the Spirit of God descending like a dove and lighting on him. And a voice from heaven said, 'This is my Son, whom I love; with him I am well pleased.'   Matthew 3.13–16

Empowered People

At his baptism Jesus was empowered for leadership and ministry. There is much more that could be said about the baptism narrative, but for our purposes this will suffice. We must not underestimate the significance of this empowering in Christ's leadership formation, or the importance for his followers to undergo a similar anointing of power for ministry leadership. Indeed Jesus said just this: 'You will receive power when the Holy Spirit comes upon you; and you will be my witnesses…' (Acts 1.8)—words fulfilled at Pentecost and beyond (Acts 2ff), as the Spirit was poured out on the church. We are told to ask and keep on asking (Luke 11.13, Eph 5.18) for the Spirit to fill and equip us.

When it comes to leadership formation, it is important therefore that those responsible for choosing new leaders look for evidence of the Spirit's power in the lives of those emerging. This is true for both (lay) leaders within a local church, as well as those responsible for the selection of clergy. They should be looking for the Spirit's fruit (Gal 5.22ff) and many of his gifts (as in Romans 12.6–9 and 1 Cor 12.8–11) plus a good mix of both humility and authority as they 'live by the Spirit' (Gal 5.16). To ask anything less of leaders not only aims too low but also fails to do justice to the example Jesus has set for us.

To ask anything less of leaders fails to do justice to the example Jesus has set for us

Is Spirit-empowered Leadership Enough?

Imagine that Jesus' baptism experience happened to you. You are baptized and the Father speaks from heaven and the Spirit comes upon you like a dove. I think after that I would feel well prepared for leadership! I would be saying, 'Let's go. Let's get on with it. Now I'm full of the Spirit!'

Is that what happened to Jesus? Did he launch straight into Spirit-empowered ministry? No. In fact, quite the opposite. More preparation was needed. For this the Spirit led Jesus *into the desert* until he was fully ready to be released as a leader. We will see that the Spirit allowed Jesus to engage in four specific discipline battles whilst fasting in the desert. These experiences were an important part of Christ's own leadership formation *before* he began his three years of proclaiming and demonstrating the kingdom of God. I argue that we too, as disciples of Jesus, must face similar battles.

Question for Reflection

- Do you need to review your understanding of the Spirit—as one who might lead you into desert-like places?

3

The Battle for the Will

> Then Jesus was led by the Spirit into the desert to be tempted by the devil. After fasting for forty days and forty nights he was hungry.
>
> Matthew 4.1–2

After his baptism, Jesus is 'led by the Spirit' from the Jordan area 'into the desert' (4.1). The contrast between the two areas could not be greater.

The Desert

The Jordan Valley is a beautiful and attractive geographical plain, made fresh and fertile by the irrigation of the river. This is where John was baptizing people (3.13) and where Jesus was baptized (3.15). The Israel desert, however, is sun-scorched, brown and barren—hot by day, cold by night. Would the Holy Spirit lead someone into a wild place like this? Yes, for a season. For Jesus, the season was 40 days and nights.

Fasting in the Desert

As the Spirit leads Jesus into this place, Matthew the author anticipates what is to come by saying that Jesus is going 'to be tempted by the devil' (v 1). But notice that the three temptations that Christ experiences do not happen immediately. In fact, they come *at the end* of the 40 days. This is significant. So what was happening for the first 40 days? All we are told is that 'he was fasting' and naturally after 40 days 'he was hungry' (v 2).

We often race on from verse 2 to verse 3 of this passage, but let us rest for a while in verse 2 because it is crucial to the text, for it describes what Jesus was doing for the bulk of his time in the desert. It is also important because the so-called 'temptations' emerge out of his fasting. If Jesus had not been fasting, it is unlikely that he would have experienced these temptations, engaged in the various battles and been so well prepared for ministry. So, verse 2, Jesus was fasting. Instead of eating, he was praying.

Fasting in the Bible

Jesus' fasting is not novel or unique. In Jewish history fasting was fairly commonplace. We know that Moses (Exod 24.18; 34.28), David (2 Sam 1.12;

12.1–23), Elijah (1 Kings 19.8), Esther (Esther 4.1–17), and prophets such as Daniel (Dan 9.1–19) and Joel (Joel 1.14; 2.12, 15) either fasted themselves or encouraged it. In the New Testament we are told that, as well as Jesus and John the Baptist, the prophetess Anna (Luke 2.37) and the apostle Paul (Acts 9.9; 13.1–3; 14.23) fasted. There is good historical precedence for fasting.

The Bible does not give us a tidy list entitled 'six good reasons to fast,' but it does assume that God's people will, from time to time, fast. For example in Matthew 6.16 and 9.15 Jesus seems to mark out our time as one in which we should fast.

But why should we fast? Examples in the Bible show that fasting was normally done for a clear purpose:

As a Mark of Humility
'Yet when they were ill, I put on sackcloth and humbled myself with fasting' (Psalm 35.13).

As Part of Worship
Anna 'never left the temple but worshipped night and day, fasting and praying' (Luke 2.37).

Augustine of Hippo taught that believers should fast before they take Holy Communion and, of course, many attenders at early morning Communion services do not have breakfast until after their worship.[8]

As a Mark of Repentance
'Even now' declares the Lord, 'return to me with all your heart, with fasting and weeping and mourning' (Joel 2.12); fasting is here a sign of wanting to change.

When Choosing and Commissioning Leaders
'While they were worshipping the Lord and fasting, the Holy Spirit said, "Set apart for me Barnabas and Saul for the work to which I have called them"' (Acts 13.2–3).

For Deliverance from Satanic Oppression
Jesus replied, 'This kind can only come out by prayer and fasting' (Mark 9.29).

For Healing
'Yet when they were ill, I put on sackcloth and humbled myself with fasting' (Psalm 35.13).

Simply Out of Obedience
'When you fast...' (Matthew 6.3).

Other specific reasons for fasting include for intercessory prayer, guidance, and even physical well-being. (The detoxifying aspect of fasting should not be overlooked!)

We are not told why Jesus was fasting. However, this experience in the desert seems to be deliberately planned at the start of his public ministry and to be crucial for Jesus' leadership formation, so it is likely that the purpose of his fasting was to finally prepare him for ministry, and especially to discipline his *will*.

When I abstain from food, it only takes a few hours before my body wants more. That desire for food becomes stronger and stronger. Then, as nutrition experts have found, the craving begins to disappear as your body realizes it is not going to be fed (although at different times it returns—sometimes with vengeance!). How do we not give in to this craving for food? The answer is in *the will*.

The Will

The 'will' is the decision-making part of us. It is the part that says 'yes' and 'no' to things. We use the word 'will' frequently. For instance, we talk of having *will-power*, the ability to stand firm in the face of temptation or challenge. We use the phrase *strong-willed* to describe someone with the inner strength to be disciplined and controlled. The word *will* also refers to a legal document that contains the decisions someone has made about what happens to their estate after they die. The will, then, is about decision-making.

Jesus and Fasting

As Jesus fasted, he entered into a battle for his will. He was a human being like you and me; as the fast went on, there must have been times when he felt like giving up and stopping. He would have felt weak, and his emotions probably went up and down. But he triumphed, with the help of the Spirit.

Having won the battle for the will in the desert *before* he began his public ministry, his life *during* his ministry was founded on a disciplined will. We know that during his ministry he would pray regularly, often getting up early, that he would be disciplined about investing time in training disciples and, no doubt, he would be regularly reading and meditating on the Jewish Scriptures. I expect that this battle for the will significantly prepared him for all this. His disciplined will, and resultant disciplined lifestyle, provided a structure to his day that then resourced him to lead a life flexible to the promptings of the Spirit and the circumstances presented to him.

*Jesus' disciplined lifesty[l]
provided a structure to [h]
day that resourced him t[o]
lead a life flexible to the
promptings of the Spirit*

It is speculation, but I would not be surprised if the apostle Paul went through a similar experience during his three years of spiritual formation in Arabia and Damascus (Gal 1.17–18).

Christ's triumphant battle for the will was fought in co-operation with the Holy Spirit. After all, it was the Spirit who led him into the desert to engage in this battle. It was the Spirit's fruit of self-control that he was displaying (Gal 5.23). It is the same for us, especially because we are weakened by sinfulness in ways that Jesus never was. Learning to have a disciplined will is not something that we do on our own, divorced from the Spirit. The Spirit wants to lead us into this battle so that together we might have control over our will.

Fasting Today

Many Christian leaders today find it difficult to achieve a balance between being proactive and reactive in ministry. I want to 'walk in the Spirit' and be able to respond to the things that the Spirit leads me into each day, and yet I realize that I also need to be proactive in taking the initiative and in starting new things, as the Spirit guides. This proactive-reactive balance needs to be birthed out of a life of prayerful discipline, and I find that the best way for that to happen is for me to have a healthy framework for each week and each day, providing structure within which there is a fair degree of flexibility. This framework, however, can only really be achieved if we have a disciplined will. In short, we need, like Christ, to have co-operated with the Spirit in the battle for the will.

Fasting is crucial here, for

> If we desire the Holy Spirit to have control of our lives then we must let him subdue our basic passions…The most basic passion is food…Fasting is the means by which we can gain control over this most basic passion.[9]

That is why I normally fast one day a week as part of my rhythm for the week, and in the context of the prayer life of my local church. Not only does it help me in my prayers, it is also part of the framework of my life and helps me submit my will to God.

But the battle for the will is fought on many fronts, not just fought through fasting. For instance, setting the alarm clock to get up early to pray and meditate on the Scriptures is, for many, part of the battle for the will. If we cannot make time somewhere in the day for daily devotion to God, then maybe we have not yet won through in this battle. However, for Jesus at this point fasting was the main battle-front and I expect that it is the same for many of us.

Fasting and Leadership Formation

In the eighteenth century, John Wesley had a number of criteria that Methodist ministers needed to fulfil before selection for leadership. One was that they fasted for at least two days each week.[10] Perhaps Wesley knew something about leadership formation that we have lost today.

Perhaps Wesley knew something about leadership formation that we have lost today

As I write, I am challenged to go deeper into this. I encourage you to allow the Holy Spirit to take you into the battle for the will. Be open to his guidance, especially in the area of fasting. If you have practical questions about how you might begin to fast, turn on to the Appendix, which looks at some practical fasting issues.

The battle for the will is about knowing and agreeing that God wants us to be disciplined people with good patterns in our lives that will help us be more effective followers of Jesus and servants of his good news. It is not just about trying harder. We are called to a disciplined life *in co-operation with this Spirit*. It is an ongoing battle for the will, in which we find victory as we rely on the Holy Spirit.

It is an ongoing battle for the will, in which we find victory as we rely on the Holy Spirit

In some ways this battle goes on throughout life and yet there is a decisive battle that needs to be fought, the kind Jesus fought in the desert through fasting, that prepares us for this life of disciplined discipleship.

So, do not run from the desert when the Spirit leads you there. It is a place of struggle, of growth and of victory which forms us in his image.

Questions for Reflection

- How has the battle for the will found expression in your life?
- What fronts do you find it easier to battle on?
- What fronts do you find it harder to battle on?
- What is your experience, to date, of fasting?
- What practical things can you do to grow in success in the battlefront of fasting?

The Battle for the Body

4

The tempter came to him and said, 'If you are the Son of God, tell these stones to become bread.' Jesus answered, 'It is written: "People do not live on bread alone, but on every word that comes from the mouth of God."'

Matthew 4.1–4

The next three battles emerge as a consequence of the first one. The first battle is mainly within your self; your 'will' is so central to who you are. Once you have established that your will is under some kind of discipline, then the devil, in my experience, begins to get a little worried. So he fights back. This is what he did with Jesus, as he engaged in the subsequent battles for the body, the mind and the soul.

If you are not already finding victory in the battle for the will then it is virtually impossible to triumph in the battle for the body, mind, or soul. The will, as we have seen, is foundational to spiritual formation and to the other three discipline battles. This chapter explores the first of these supplementary battles: the battle for the body.

Tested by the Devil

The devil comes to Jesus when he is feeling physically, and maybe emotionally and mentally, weak. Have you noticed it is the same for us? When I am tired, run down, or stressed, I am vulnerable to the temptations and testings.

'If you really are the Son of God…' says the devil. Satan is trying to put Jesus on the back foot, so that he ends up using the privileges that go with his status for wrong purposes. It is often the same for us. Sometimes I find a voice inside that begins with my identity: 'you're God's son…part of God's family…God wants good things for you…so God won't mind if you indulge in…'[11]

The particular issue here, of course, is bread. Remember that Jesus is ravenous and the devil now offers him a solution to his hunger: turn these stones into bread. This would have been a very tempting proposition, as some of the stones in the desert would have looked rather like bread in both shape and size. What the devil is doing is challenging him to enter the battle for the body.

Body: Temple of the Holy Spirit

When we today enter this particular arena we are often hindered by some of the church's teaching about the human body. Since the early days of Christianity, the church has often gone to one of two extremes in its ideas about the human body. Both emerge out of a false sense of dualism (evident in much Greek philosophical thinking) that divorces the physical from the spiritual. This kind of teaching says that within the human person God is only interested in and 'saves' the soul and/or spirit, not the body.

One extreme develops this by saying that the human body must therefore be sinful. If this is right, we must suppress the body, beat it, deny it. Church history is full of people who have tried to live this way, most of them fairly unsuccessfully. There is a place for denial of the body, but that is not to suggest that the body is sinful. This is not the teaching of Scripture. Commentators on 1 Corinthians think that there were a number of so-called 'spiritual' women in the Corinthian church who held to this kind of teaching and so were denying sex to their husbands. How does Paul handle this? By saying 'do not deprive each other' (1 Cor 7.3–5). He is clearly coming against this kind of false dualism.

The other extreme teaches that the human body is not sinful, just unimportant. If this is the case, then it does not matter what you do with your body. Enjoy whatever carnal pleasures come your way. Again, some Corinthian Christians seem to have supported this view. Paul deals with it head on in 1 Corinthians 6.12–16, tackling the question of food and sex, saying that the way we look after our bodies is important. Why? Because our 'bodies are temples of the Holy Spirit' (1 Cor 6.19).

As we consider the battle for the body we need to be aware that many of us will subconsciously subscribe to some kind of physical/spiritual dualism that can be unhelpful. To counter this we should remember that each one has been created by God as a unity, as a whole person. Following Jesus will involve every aspect of life.

Many of us will subconsciously subscribe to some kind of physical / spiritual dualism

This means that we must not neglect the body; we must look after it and learn to master it; this is the battle for the body. Neither must we treat the body like a god, something which many in our contemporary culture seem to do, obsessed as we are with dieting, beauty products, plastic surgery and gaining 'the perfect physique.'

Three Issues

What kind of issues confront us in this battle for the body? Here are three, relevant to life in the early years of the 21st Century.

First, *food.* When Jesus was in the desert the battle for the body was fought over the issue of food. He was fasting and hungry and was tempted to eat, which is not in itself wrong. Eating is a good thing (Gen 1.29), but when the Spirit has led us into a fast it becomes a matter of discipline.

Furthermore, when we face this battlefront we may be confronted with questions concerning the kind of food we eat; whether we are having a balanced diet; eating good quality food, or 'junk' food; eating too much; having too many fatty foods, or perhaps putting on too much weight. We might need to ask whether we are taking in too many stimulants, such as alcohol or coffee. Who is in charge of your body? The Spirit-led you, or your body?[12] God wants it to be the Spirit-led you.

A second area is *physical fitness.* Whilst we are not meant to be obsessed with our bodies, we need to keep fit and healthy. God has granted us a physical body that we need to take care of. I am aware from my studies on David Watson that despite his many achievements, he died at the young age of 50, having worked too hard, having drunk too much coffee, and probably lived with too much stress in his life.[13]

Fighting on this battlefront will involve consciously taking care of our bodies. When taking short journeys we might try to walk rather than taking the car. We might decide to exercise more; perhaps swim regularly or do stretching exercises.

A third issue is our *sexuality.* Our sexuality is linked with our hormones and emotions and is a very strong drive in many people. I do not need to rehearse the massive confusion and debate in the Anglican Church at the moment, and we are not alone in this.

Most couples in the UK, and many Christian couples, experiment with full sexual expression before marriage. Some dabble outside of marriage. Many men are addicted to pornography. Others are confused about homosexuality and whether it is morally and theologically acceptable. This is a real battle-ground! This writer, holding to the primacy of Scripture as God's revelation, believes that the Bible describes a clear, simple and wonderful way to victory in this battlefront, namely through preserving sexual expression within the boundaries of a marriage between a man and woman. Yet this is not always easy, for the single person, for those of a homosexual orientation, or even sometimes for married people. It requires self-control, hence the need for victory in the initial battle for the will. Without this, there will be many defeats.

> Fighting on this battlefront will raise searching issues in our sex lives. It will require us to co-operate with the Spirit of God rather than constantly falling into temptation, feeling confused or guilty. The good news is that the Spirit wants to help us (Rom 8.26; 2 Cor 12.10).

Whilst there is always work to do in all these areas throughout our lives, God wants us to have won a decisive battle for the body, so we can proceed with confidence in life and leadership. It is easy to neglect this battle for the body; but leaders who do walk in a minefield.

Word and Master

Two final things on the body. First, the *word of God*. When Jesus replies to Satan's question (that he should turn the stones into bread) he quotes from Deuteronomy 8.3. By citing this text, Christ is actually saying: 'God desires the whole person to be fed, not just the stomach.' This other food, Jesus says, is 'every word that comes from the mouth of God,' a phrase shortened elsewhere to 'the word of God.'

Jesus is therefore saying that to win the battle for the body, we must be regularly feeding, chewing and digesting God's word, the Bible. It is to be a regular part of our lives in the same way that taking meals is a normal part of the rhythm of life.

Secondly, there is an issue about *master and servant*. God has given us bodies to help us do what he has called us to do. The human body is supposed to be the servant, not the master.

This thought neatly summarizes this chapter on the battle for the body, because we know we have won this battle if we can positively answer the question: are you the servant of your body, or does your body serve you?

Questions for Reflection

- Who is the master, and who is the servant—your body, or the Spirit-led you?

- Your body is the 'temple of the Holy Spirit.' Are you taking care of God's temple?

- Go back to the section about food, physical fitness, and sex (p 13–14). In what areas are you challenged to make some changes?

The Battle for the Mind

> Then the devil took him to the holy city and had him stand on the highest point of the temple. 'If you are the Son of God,' he said, 'throw yourself down. For it is written: "he will command his angels concerning you, and they will lift you up in their hands, so that you will not strike your foot against a stone."' Jesus answered him, 'It is also written: "Do not put the Lord your God to the test."'   Matthew 4.5–7

Having won the battle for will and the battle for the body, Jesus now faces a third battle: *the battle for the mind*. Our thinking is crucial if we are to be effective Christian disciples and leaders. 'Be careful how you think; your life is shaped by your thoughts' (Prov 4.23, GNB).

Our Thinking

I still remember the scene. I was seven years old and standing on the landing at the top of the stairs at home. Fixed to the wall was a large mirror and there I was, looking directly into it and staring at myself, looking deep inside myself. As I did so, a thought came into my mind that I had never ever considered before. It made me feel both good and naughty at the same time. It was one of those watershed moments where things will never be the same again. The thought was this: no-one else can know my thoughts. I do not have to share them. I can keep them to myself and nobody needs to know what I am thinking.

Since then I have discovered that one other person knows my thoughts—God himself (Psalm 94.11), which is both comforting and challenging. But for most of us, we are pleased that people do not know our thoughts, because if they did, we would be terribly embarrassed!

One of my wife's favourite films is *What Women Want*. Mel Gibson stars as a man who for a time can hear the thoughts of women around him. There is much amusement as he begins to understand the way women think (something most men would love to know!). This light-hearted film does, however, raise a serious question, concerning human thought and thought-processes. What is going on inside our heads? And can the Holy Spirit help us in this arena?

The Scriptures are clear that God does want to be involved in our thinking. It is a huge battle-field and he wants us to triumph.

The apostle Paul wrote to believers in Rome:

> Do not conform any longer to the pattern of this world. But be transformed by the renewing of your mind. Then you will be able to test and approve what God's will is... (Romans 12.2).

Our minds can be renewed. Indeed this instruction is left for us because God wants to help us in this process of the renewing of our minds. Thinking in a mature, 'godly' manner is so important that Paul wrote similarly to the Corinthians:

> Brothers and sisters, stop thinking like children. In regard to evil be infants, but in your thinking be adults (1 Corinthians 14.20).

Prayer, Opportunity, Action

But *how* might God influence our thinking? The answer is that God does not just *do* it (that is, force it on us). It is a process and therefore part of leadership formation. As ever, he wants us to work in co-operation with the Spirit. That is why, as we have been discovering, it is important to be full of the Holy Spirit (to ask and keep on asking) and have won the battle for the will.

If we are serious about serving Christ and being effective in leadership, we should be aware that God's kingdom is transformative in nature (see Luke 4.16–21) and that we are called to co-operate with him in bringing positive change to all sorts of people and situations. As we pray for this, so we should be expectant that God-given opportunities will arise. We then need to be courageous and turn those opportunities into action. For some of us, this 'prayer–opportunity–action' paradigm involves a whole new way of thinking. Here are three examples of how it could work.

If we pray to be more effective in evangelism (that is, telling people about Christ), we should expect that God will bring across our paths people who want to hear the good news. Our job is to recognize them and use the opportunity. If we ask God to be involved in praying for people who are ill, we need to look out for sick people. They will come our way. When they do, we must seize the opportunity. If we pray to become even better at our job (whatever the field of work), we should expect God to put us in situations which stretch us, so we have the opportunity to improve and excel. God is much more willing to answer our prayers than most of us imagine (Eph 3.20) and he wants our thinking to increasingly reflect this.

Enemy Tactics

When we begin to take discipleship seriously and start to think and look for the answer to our prayers, the devil realizes that he has a new set of 'trouble-makers' around and he too begins to bring opposition our way (see Eph 6.11–12; 1 Peter 5.8). Yet God, who is sovereign, can use this and turn it into a victory (as described in the inspirational story of Joseph, see Gen 50.20).

We see this particularly in Matthew 4.5–7 as the enemy tempts Jesus by taking him to the highest point of temple. 'Throw yourself down' Jesus is told. Jesus could have done so and angels *would have* caught him. But what would be the point? Perhaps Jesus might have enjoyed some kind of self-indulgent thrill from the experience or perhaps it would be to test his power.

Clearly the first of these is wrong; divine power is not for selfish gain or pleasure, but is for the benefit of others. Jesus needed to be sure of this if he was to be effective in ministry leadership, and so do we. A simple yet important biblical principle is that God blesses us that we might bless others. If Jesus gave in at this point in his life, how else might he have manipulated the power of God in the future?

Furthermore, Jesus does not need to prove his power, and certainly not in this way. He already has the Holy Spirit dwelling in him and knows that if he is to live up to the calling of the Father, he needs to be led by the Spirit of *God*, not by the devil or any spirit of *evil*. We too need to learn this lesson, that power should be used carefully and wisely.

Misuse and Good Use of Scripture

The challenge from the devil, however, is not just about (mis)using the power that is made available to us through the Spirit; the battle for the mind also lies at the very heart of the faith, in the realm of revelation. For Satan challenges Jesus to do something unhelpful on the basis of *holy Scripture*, God's revealed word (Psalm 119.43, 89; 2 Tim 3.16). He takes two verses from Psalm 91 and attempts to twist them for his own ends. This is one of his tactics in the community of faith (2 Tim 4.1–5; 2 Peter 2.1–3).

Jesus is able to respond because he has a grasp of *the totality* of Scripture, knowing that Psalm 91 needs to be placed alongside other passages such as Deuteronomy 7, 'Do not put the Lord your God to the test,' in order to have a full biblical perspective.

This is how Jesus wins the battle: not by knowing the odd verse from the Bible, but by knowing the whole of Scripture, and having a good grasp of its themes. He is then able to bring relevant Scriptures to mind at the appropriate time.[14] This understanding allows him to know when Scripture is used in a manipulative way, that is, to say what someone wants it to say.

In the battle for the mind, therefore, leaders need to know Scripture, like Jesus, in such a way that we think, live and act in accordance with it. As we think in this way we will begin to understand (sometimes instinctively) when Scripture is being mishandled.

Having this kind of broad biblical perspective is crucial for leaders in the church today facing many of the current debates. We need to know Scripture and use it wisely in the battles we face.

The Sword of the Spirit

Scripture is described by the apostle Paul as the sword of the Spirit (Eph 6.17) to be used on the various battlefields of life. The context within which the Spirit's sword appears is Ephesians 6.10–18. This is a famous passage reminding us that we are in a battle (v 12); the battle is not against people, but against the devil and his forces (v 12). In this battle God wants us to stand (vv 13, 14) and as Christ's followers, we must wear and use the armour given us (v 11, v 13). Most of the armour is defensive, except the feet clothed with the gospel (to advance), and the sword of the Spirit (v 17, to fight).

The battle against the enemy is fought on a number of fronts,[15] although we are looking at the four main personal discipline battles in this book. The battle for the mind is crucial if we are to be effective leaders, for when we think Christ-like thoughts, we live Christ-like lives. The devil hates it when people's minds are renewed and they begin to think God's way, resulting in Christian action.

Satan winces when people think scripturally about their marriages. He is disgusted when people begin to realize that all their money and assets are from God and treat them as such. He rages when we decide to stop seeing those troublesome neighbours as a problem and decide to pray for them, be kind to them, invite them in for coffee, and ask if we can help them. This is practical spiritual warfare.[16]

Thinking Christianly is what the battle for the mind is all about, and it is often aided by fasting.[17] It is a crucial component of leadership formation. Through co-operation with the Spirit, this battle can and must be won.

Questions for Reflection

- Is there one particular area of your life where you are challenged to think differently? Ask God to change your way of thinking, and then lead you into opportunities where that new thinking can result in practical action.

- A sword is a weapon that can be used for good and ill. Timothy is commended for being one 'who carefully handles the word of truth' (2 Tim 2.15). How can you improve your handling of God's sword—the Scriptures?

The Battle for the Soul   6

> Again, the devil took him to a very high mountain and showed him all the kingdoms of the world and their splendour. 'All this I will give you,' he said, 'if you bow down and worship me.' Jesus said to him, 'Away from me, Satan! For it is written: "Worship the Lord your God, and serve him only."' Then the devil left him, and angels came and attended him.
>
> Matthew 4.8–11

The fourth and final discipline battle is the battle for the soul. Towards the end of his fast, Jesus is taken to a high place to observe all the kingdoms of the world and is told: 'All this I will give to you.' What an offer!

Gifts Before Time

This raises a deeper theological question concerning the devil's ownership or possession of all kingdoms of the world. There are two views here:

i   that the kingdoms rightfully belong to God but for a time are in the possession of the devil, or

ii   that they have always belonged to God, and Satan is trying to give away what does not belong to him. (Readers may wish to refer to commentaries if they wish to follow up this and other issues[18]).

I personally prefer the first view, but whichever one holds, these kingdoms, in the future, if not now, are going to belong to Christ in any event.[19] Revelation 11.15 is very specific about this when it says: 'The kingdom of this world has become the kingdom of our Lord and of his Christ.' And Jesus knows this. So he is being offered now something that is going to be his in the future. It is offered early, before time.

The devil often tempts like this. He tempts us with things early, things before time. Abraham is told by God that his offspring will inherit the land of Canaan (Gen 12.7), but Abraham is kept waiting and so eventually takes his wife's concubine and has a child through her (Gen 16). This is not, however, God's plan and later his elderly wife Sarah gives birth to the child of promise (Gen 21). Abraham was tempted to take now what was to be his in the future.

And there were resulting difficulties and problems that emerged (Genesis 21ff) because he tried to receive the good things of God before time.

In today's culture we see this illustrated in sex before marriage. Sex is a beautiful gift from God, designed to be shared in the context of marriage. To practice sex before marriage is not a despicable or unforgivable sin. But it is to take a gift early, before time, and is to be discouraged.

In Matthew 4, Jesus is offered power by the devil, power before time

In Matthew 4, Jesus is offered power by the devil, power before time. In order to receive his power *now* Jesus is told by the devil that he needs to 'Bow down and worship me.' Jesus has to give his soul to the devil. This is the fourth and last battle: the battle for the soul.

The Soul

Throughout history there has been a philosophical and theological debate about the nature of the 'soul' and its distinction from the spirit, body, mind or emotions. I am not going to enter this debate in any depth, except to define the 'soul' for our purposes as that part of the human being that reaches out in worship. So when we sing the great hymn, 'Praise *my soul* the king of heaven' we are encouraging our soul to offer worship to God, which is natural, right and proper.

Jesus knew that the battle for the soul was about worship. That is why his reply to the devil (where he again cites Scripture, using the sword of the Spirit) is about worship: 'For it is written: "Worship the Lord your God, and serve him only."'

So the battle for the soul is about worship. It is about who or what we will worship.

Worship

Worship is what we were created for. This is why the first commandment (in Exodus 20) is about worship, for it is fundamental to our human design. We all worship something—if not God, then something else. At the heart of the revelation of God is the command for human beings to worship Almighty God and 'have no other gods' (Exodus 20.3).

All of us worship, or are tempted to worship things other than God, things like money, possessions, selfish dreams or other people. As we worship these things, they become 'other gods' or 'idols' for us. That is why we need to keep on repenting, worshipping and realigning our focus on God.

If Jesus had given in and accepted the kingdoms now, he would simply have been feeding selfish human desires. Giving in would have meant serving the devil, and losing the battle for the soul.[20] This is a serious matter, and we need to realize that it is the same for us. So often we think it is not so great an issue if we give in to our own selfishness and allow things to become 'gods' in our lives. But here it is made patently clear that by doing this we are not just serving our 'self' but in fact the devil himself.

o often we think it is not so great an issue if we give in to our own selfishness

As Jesus fasted, then, one of the key issues he had to face was: who will he worship? As you and I fast, this question will come up for us too. If leaders win through in this area, it will stand us in good stead for the future and can provide a significant reference point when we feel low. It is easy to be tempted to give up, but the important thing is that we stand (Eph 6.11ff). This raises a fundamental question that all Christians, especially leaders, need to have positively answered: will you commit yourself to worship God, for the rest of your life?

It is rather like the first (and foundational) question asked of a couple standing in church to be married. They are not asked if they like each other, love each other, even fancy each other. They are simply asked 'will you?' 'Will you take x to be your husband / wife?' And the appropriate reply, of course, is 'I will'!

The battle for the soul is, like the other battles, linked to the battle for the will. It is about saying 'I will' worship and serve God, and 'I will not' worship and serve the devil.

Losing the World; Gaining Life

The cost for Christ was to give up the world. We too are called to give up 'the world' with its offers, values and the attractiveness of its power. The irony, however, is that if we win the battle for the soul, the good things of life will eventually come to us in any event. Jesus would one day receive all the kingdoms of the world and so it was worth the wait. And it is the same for us, for there are great things to receive in the age to come (Mark 10.30). By denying ourselves and giving our souls to God, we actually find that we gain life (John 10.10)—partly now and fully when Jesus returns. This is exactly what Jesus taught, through lessons learned in the desert:

By denying ourselves and giving our souls to God, we actually find that we gain life

- 'Those who would come after me must deny themselves and take up their cross and follow me. For those who want to save their lives will lose them, but those who lose their lives for me will gain them. What good will it be for you to gain the whole world, yet forfeit your soul?' (Matthew 16.24).

- 'Take my yoke upon you and learn from me, for I am gentle and humble in heart, and you will find rest for your souls' (Matthew 11.29).

The battle for the soul is a battle that the Spirit of God wants to help you win. So, take up the sword of the Spirit and do not be afraid to triumph in this battle arena. Be encouraged by the words God spoke to the great warrior Joshua, just before he went to war:

'Have I not commanded you? Be strong and courageous. Do not be terrified; do not be discouraged, for the Lord your God will be with you wherever you go' (Joshua 1.9).

Questions for Reflection

- Do you have 'other gods' that compromise your soul? Is there a spiritual director or friend in whom you can confide, to confess and deal with these things?

- In what areas are you tempted to enjoy God's blessing before time? Ask the Spirit for help.

- Are you prepared to give up power, so as to win the battle for the soul?

Conclusion: Freedom & Discipline 7

The Integrated Life of the Leader

We have considered the four personal battles that the Spirit of God wants us to enter in order to triumph and be formed for leadership as disciples of Jesus. The way that the Spirit takes Jesus into these battles is through the discipline of fasting, and this will often be the way for us. This is not to say that there are not other ways, other disciplines. But fasting is one of the main ones and it is one that we too often ignore to our peril today.

Jesus emerges ready for ministry leadership and displays an integrated life, combining both freedom and discipline. This is the life we need and the life that should develop if we are truly led by the Spirit.

The apostle Paul understood this, so much so that when he writes about the Holy Spirit to the young church leader Timothy, he describes the Spirit as

> ...a spirit of power, of love and of self-discipline (2 Tim 1.7).

Power and love are intrinsic to his nature, and together bring a *freedom* to our lives. But we must not forget that he is also the Spirit 'of self-*discipline*,' as we have been considering in this book.

Freedom

As we are formed for leadership, we need the freedom that the Spirit brings. This comes from Holy Spirit baptism and knowing the ongoing work of the Spirit of life in our lives (Rom 8.2ff). He is the Spirit of liberation (Luke 4.18), for us and others. We need to be flexible, attentive and responsive to his guidance, for 'the Lord is the Spirit, and where the Spirit of the Lord is, there is freedom' (2 Cor 3.17–18).

It is possible to be a church leader and not really to have grasped the 'glorious freedom of the children of God' (Rom 8.21). We all need to continue to learn from Christ who was so led by the Spirit of freedom that he could say with sincerity that 'he only does what he sees his Father doing' (John 5.19).

Yet Christ was also disciplined. He had an integrated lifestyle that allowed *both* elements of freedom and discipline to shape his ministry and leadership. We need the same—freedom *and* discipline.

Discipline

We live in a world that knows little about discipline. Perhaps athletes are one of the few groups of people who know something about it, training long and hard to be successful. Unfortunately, even athletes are sometimes tempted to take short-cuts.

Discipline is about training yourself for the long-term. It is about seeing the *future* benefit. Many find this kind of outlook difficult today as the culture in which we live seems to champion short-termism, being obsessed with the *present*. We have instant coffee, instant food, instant credit, instant access—instant everything! This rubs off on us all. I get cross when internet downloads take too long, or when I have to wait for an elevator.

I also think we are part of a church that knows little more than the world about discipline. Fasting, as we are seeing, is foundational for Christian discipline and yet, according to Richard Foster, there was no Christian book published in the West on fasting between 1861 and 1954.[21] That is very telling. Since then there have been some helpful works printed (although very little from Anglicans).[22] Who is going to educate the church about the many benefits of fasting?

We need to learn again how to be led by the Spirit, how to be formed for leadership and how to fast.

Going into the Desert

May I encourage you, then, to allow the Spirit of God, the Spirit of freedom *and* discipline, to lead you into the desert. There is a risk, but the benefits are great.

It is rather like the children in C S Lewis' *The Lion, the Witch and the Wardrobe*. They were staying with an elderly gentleman in a large house for the long summer holidays. As they opened a large wardrobe in the spare room they discovered a whole new world of adventure. They could have chosen not to enter, and they may still have had a reasonable holiday in the house. But once they had been into this world of Narnia, they could not imagine life without those adventures. In the same way, as we fast we will be led into a world of adventure, a world of battles, challenges and opportunities that will form us well for leadership. So do not miss out. Open the door. Enter in.

Appendix

Practicalities of Fasting

If we want to fast, where do we start? It is the Nike Corporation who have the logo: 'Just do it.' Maybe that is a good starting point—to simply begin and see where the Spirit leads.

Practically, drink plenty, either water or perhaps some juice, for the body can only last a few days without fluids. As with most disciplines, be realistic, perhaps start by fasting for just for one or two meals. For the last four years at St Chad's Church in Sheffield we have set aside Thursday as 'Prayer Day.' There are a number of different prayer gatherings, some formal, some informal. We encourage folk to set aside special time to pray for church and community, and some people choose to fast over lunch. You could try something similar.

I am a novice in some aspects of fasting. I do fast regularly, as part of my worship (like Anna, Luke 2.37), and for intercession, but I have no experience to date of long-term fasting. If this is an area you would like to explore, I would recommend Foster's chapter in *Celebration of Discipline* (see footnote 21) and the excellent Grove booklet by David Bolster and Anna de Lange entitled *Fasting—A Fresh Look at an Old Discipline* (see footnote 9).

Purpose of Fasting

Many Christians want to know the purpose of fasting, especially if they feel they have managed fine without it. Here are three.

First (and foundational): it releases God's power. The Bible does not explain how and there is an element of mystery here. But the wise will perceive it. Interestingly, other religions know something of this. Buddhists, Muslims, the Yogis of India and other religions encourage fasting. They understand that humans have been created to benefit from this practice. Regrettably many Christians, who in Christ have the most amazing revelation of God, are slow to grasp this.

Second (and this is the basic premise of this book): it will launch us into battles that will prepare for effective leadership. I am convinced of this. This kind of fasting is mainly for personal growth, allowing the Spirit of freedom and discipline to be at work deep within our wills, bodies, minds and souls.

Third: fasting is normally focussed, that is, for a particular purpose, as we saw in chapter three. As well as fasting for your own benefit, you can fast for others, perhaps as part of your intercessory prayers. Some will fast for a particular person or situation. When their body says 'Time to eat' they say 'Time to pray.' People fast as an act of repentance, personal or corporate. Corporate fasting can also be used for calling out to God to avert disaster.[23] St Basil (329–379) rightly said that fasting is not abstaining from food only; it is first of all 'alienation from evil,' that is, abstaining from sin.'[24]

Other Kinds of Fast

Fasting does not need to be confined to the realm of food. The Bible talks about fasting from sex[25] or alcohol.[26] During Lent, many give up coffee or chocolate. Sometimes we can see these things as frivolous or unimportant, but as you practice them you do actually begin to enter the realms of the first battle, the battle for the will. And that is good—assuming you triumph! However, do not stop there; allow yourselves to proceed into the next three battles.

Notes

1   Greek: *diabolos* (devil; literally: 'slanderer'); Aramaic: *satan* (satan; literally: 'adversary'). I agree with R T France, that 'The devil... appears in Matthew as a real and powerful rival, the one whose authority is threatened by Jesus' inauguration of the kingdom of heaven (12.25–29; 13.19, 39; 16.23).' See R T France, *Matthew*, Tyndale Commentary (Leicester: IVP, 1985) p 98.

2   For further reading see, for example, J C Thomas, 'The Devil, Disease and Deliverance: James 5.14–16,' *Journal of Pentecostal Theology*, No 2, 1993, pp 25–50—especially bibliography at refs 1–4.

3   For a good introductory booklet on leadership, see Richard Williams and Mark Tanner, *Developing Visionary Leadership* (Grove Renewal booklet R 17).

4   The phrase 'leadership formation' is relatively new to the UK, picking up the established language of 'spiritual formation' but applying it particularly to Christian leadership (lay or ordained).

5   R T France hints at this more positive reading of the text when he states: 'Satan's intention was, no doubt, to persuade Jesus to do wrong, but the initiative was with God…' (*op cit*), p 96.

6   As noted by Hagner: 'The baptism of Jesus…serves as a kind of transition between the work of preparation and (his) appearance upon the center stage…' and 'The baptism and temptation of Jesus belong together.' Donald A Hagner, *Matthew 1–13*, Word Commentary 33A (Dallas: Word, 1993) p 54 and p 63.

7   This does not exclude Matthew's clear intention to show how Jesus fulfils the Messianic hope of the Old Testament. Note for example the symbolism of Israel's 40 years (*cf* Jesus' 40 days) in the wilderness; much use of OT Scripture—especially Deut 6–8; Israel failing to learn its desert lessons (*cf* Jesus who succeeds).

8   See 'Letters of Augustine,' *Nicene and Post-Nicene Fathers*, 1ˢᵗ Series, vol 1 (Peabody: Hendrickson, 1995) pp 302–303.

9   David Bolster and Anna de Lange, *Fasting—A Fresh Look at an Old Discipline* (Grove Spirituality booklet S 83) p 15.

10 This reflected the teaching of the Early Church, where fasting on Wednesdays and Fridays was strongly encouraged, if not obligatory for all believers. See, for example, 2ⁿᵈ Century 'The Teaching of the Apostles,' in *Ante-Nicene Fathers*, vol 7 (Peabody: Hendrickson, 1995) pp 379.

11 Interestingly it is the devil who questions Christ's sonship (vv 3 and 6) not Christ who uses it as a means of advocacy or defence. Christ is secure in his identity and does not allow his sonship to be successfully challenged. We too need to be confident that we have been adopted into the family of God (Rom 8.12–17).

12 According to St Gregory the Sinaite there are three degrees of eating: temperance, sufficiency and satiety. *Temperance* is when someone wants to eat some more food but abstains, rising from the table still somewhat hungry. *Sufficiency* is when someone eats what is needed and sufficient for normal nourishment. *Satiety* is when someone eats more than enough and is more than satisfied. See *Gleanings from Orthodox Christian Authors and the Holy Fathers*, www.orthodox.net/gleaning/fasting.html, downloaded on 29.03.05.

13 Matthew Porter, *David Watson—Evangelism, Renewal and Reconciliation* (Grove Renewal booklet R 12).

14 We see this on a number of occasions in Jesus' ministry—even when he was dying on the cross (for example Matthew 27.46)

15 These include corporate battles, fought in the context of family life, on our streets, at work, in institutions, even governments and political systems. These

are seen by some to be part of the 'rulers,' 'authorities' and 'powers' of Eph 6.12. For an interesting discussion on this, see John Stott, *Ephesians*, Bible Speaks Today Commentary (Leicester: IVP, 1979) pp 263–275.

16 This kind of practical battling is encouraged by Chrysostom: 'We are not so earnest for our own salvation, as (the devil) is for our ruin. Let us then shun him, not with words only, but also in deed.' 'Homily XIII' on Matt 4.1, *op cit*, p 83.

17 The Orthodox Elder Ephraim of Philotheou Mount Athos, helpfully says that 'Fasting causes the mind to be cleansed constantly. It whithers up every evil thought and brings healthy, godly thoughts—holy thoughts that enlighten the mind and kindle it with more zeal and spiritual fervour.' (Cited in *Gleanings from Orthodox Christian Authors and the Holy Fathers, op cit*).

18 For example, D A Hagner, *Matthew 1–13, op cit*; R T France, *Matthew, op cit*; R Gundry, *Matthew: a Commentary on his Literary and Theological Art* (Grand Rapids: Eerdmans, 2nd ed, 1994); D A Carson, *Matthew,* Expositor's Commentary Vol 8 (Grand Rapids: Zondervan, 1984); E Schweizer, *Good News according to Matthew* (London: SPCK, 1976); R Schnackenburg, *The Gospel of Matthew* (Grand Rapids: Eerdmans, English ed, 2002).

19 With France and others.

20 It would also, of course, have meant that Christ would have gone to the cross *not* as the sinless Lamb of God—and so the very salvation of the world won through the cross and resurrection would not have been achieved.

21 Richard Foster, *Celebration of Discipline* (London: Hodder and Stoughton, 1980, 1989) p 61.

22 More recently the writing of Chavda has been influential internationally in charismatic and Pentecostal circles. Whilst in no way a scholarly work, Chavda's story is persuasive. See Mahesh Chavda, *The Hidden Power of Prayer and Fasting* (Shippensburg: Destiny Image, 1998).

23 See 2 Chron 20.1–12. John Wesley's *Journal* also records that in February 1756 King George II proclaimed a national day of fasting due to a threatened French invasion. 'Every church…was more than full; and a solemn seriousness sat on every face. Surely…' (wrote Wesley) '…God heareth the prayer; and there will yet be a lengthening of our tranquillity,' which proved to be the case. See *The Works of John Wesley*, vol 2, (3rd ed, 1872; reprinted Grand Rapids: Baker, 1996) p 354.

24 Saint Basil the Great in *Nicene and Post-Nicene Fathers*, 2nd Series, vol 8 (Peabody: Hendrickson, 1995) *Prolegomena, lxi.*

25 Unless there are particular physical or emotional issues, married couples should enjoy a healthy sex life. Nevertheless, 1 Corinthians 7.5 describes a couple agreeing to abstain for a time. Why? 'So they can pray.' This is the key—turning time for playing together into time for praying together. But this should not be for too long 'so that Satan will not tempt you because of your lack of self control'!

26 Priests, in the Old Testament, were to abstain from alcohol whilst they were 'on duty' in the presence of God (see Leviticus 10.9). For some, this is a permanent fast (see the example of the Nazirites, Numbers 6.3).